2

The Majestic Spectrum

of

God's Love

By Dan Pelton, BA

April 2019

Mt. Vernon, OH

4

COPYRIGHT

The Majestic Spectrum of God's Love by Dan Pelton

Copyright© 2019

All Rights reserved. No part of this book may be reproduced in any form or by any electronic or mechanical means including information and retrievable systems without permission from the publisher/author, except by a reviewer who may quote brief passages in a review.

Published by Potpourri Publishing

Edited by Write Useful

Book cover by RebecaCovers

Printed in the United States of America

First Edition April 2019

Books> non-fiction>Christian>religious>adult

ISBN: 9781095415979

All Scripture texts quoted are from the New King James Version, copy write 1982, Thomas Nelson.

Dedication

My name may be on the by-line. It is there as a point of contact. This work may have come to light through my hands. There were times when tears came to my eyes as God allowed me to discover, see and say wonderful things. It may show some of my personality but I can rightfully lay claim to little of the work. Johannes Kepler said well, "I was merely thinking God's thoughts after him."

I was doing much of this work anyway. My wife encouraged me to do it in a way you might find useful. She greatly improved my literary skills and did much to shape this work for public consumption. My prayer is that the Spirit that moves me may move you to understand what He wants us to know.

8

Table of Contents

Name page

Getting Acquainted with the way We process God's Ideas 11

Chapter 1 Please Read This First 19

Chapter 2 The Root 25

Chapter 3 Creative Rampage 33

Chapter 4 Another Way God is Love is as Our Provider. 49

Chapter 5 Option Taken, Part One 61

Chapter 6 Option Taken , Part Two 71

Chapter 7 Unity 85

Chapter 8 Closure thoughts 93

About the Author 95

Our Invitations 97

Suggested Readings 103

Forward to Dan's book,
Or
Getting Acquainted With the Way We process God's Ideas

My husband has been studying the Gospel and God's love for most of his life, from the time he could actually read and start to process ideas. He loves the Lord, and I wish you could come sometime and throw ideas back and forth with him, as we do in our weekly home church, but lacking that ability, a book seemed the best way to share his ideas. The way he thinks, though more methodical than mine, and sometimes quite linear, compliments mine which is sometimes somewhat scattershot, and our life together spanning over four decades now has produced an increasingly more focused work. It is really our faith that has held us together all these years. It certainly wasn't our two cultures, myself being Native American/hillbilly and he being staid New England stock…

I like new thoughts and new ideas, things that make me stretch. He invents new thoughts and ideas. Perhaps that's why I love my husband so much. As a technician and a creative person, he sometimes has a way of taking ideas of others and ideas sent from the Spirit and putting them together that can be quite illuminating. To give you an example of this, long ago in college he was hashing ideas around from physics (Einstein), theology and philosophy and found what he thought was what Einstein was really trying to explain to everyone, not just math and physics but a philosophy about God. I used his idea in a couple books of mine so you may be acquainted with him already. Nevertheless, I thought to share this short treatise with you as a sort of primer on how the man thinks who is going to be writing these short books of systematic theology about the One who Creates with a Thought; about the nature and comfort of God; and warning, he is a bit more cerebral, nothing like the little devotions I write. In comparison, my devotional writings are like writing in sound or mind bites, a little here, a little there and it suddenly hits you what I am saying and falls together as a principle. He is very much like canned soup-thick, rich, sometimes needing some Water from God to blend it down to be nourishing. This concept he thought up some years ago I have paraphrased for those not of a technical bent, but it did speak to me and I hope it does for you as well. So get your imaginations revved up and come join my campfire as we start the story…

First, I want you to think of a picture of Einstein, that great old man of science. Picture him standing at a blackboard, hair askew, writing his famous relativity equation on the board. He turns to look at you to make appoint and then looks over your head and he smiles at a slightly balding man in the back with salted hair, a Bible in one hand and a tablet in the other, making notes. He sees above Dan the filmy image of a Jewish carpenter smiling at them both, rather like a proud elder Brother. Einstein nods and Dan starts inputting data. Now, let's listen in to Dan's thoughts on Einstein's hidden meanings...

In Hebrews 11:3 we read: "By faith we understand that the worlds were framed by the word of God, so that the things which are seen were not made of things which are visible." "...the things which are seen were not made of things which are visible?!" How did he know?! Look at this. Einstein has been explaining an equation that looks like this: $E=MC2$. This is the basis of nuclear energy, the atom bomb and sunshine. We are looking at a universe sprinkled with matter. So let's look for that. We rewrite the equation to read: $M=E/C2$. Let's look at what this is saying. M is for mass. We understand mass. Look in the mirror. Step on a scale. E is for energy. We know something about energy. That's what we pay the electric company for. Can you see it? Can you look at the wires and know if the energy is there? If the lights come on - it's there. If not - it's not. You can see the effects of the energy - the lights work, the fridge is cold but the energy itself is not seen. Now what about that C thing. The number that goes there is the speed of light. Speed is how far something goes in a period of time: movement in time and space. I start here and in an hour I'm 70 miles away. Do you see time? Not really. You may watch a second hand move but that is a whole set of complex goings on. And space. Do we see or even feel space? No. Things of mass may occupy some space but space isn't seen. Space is just a place to put things. Time. Space. Energy. Those are the ingredients of matter - atoms, stars, the stuff we are made of. "By faith we understand that the worlds were framed by the word of God, so that the things which are seen were not made of things which are visible." When God was ready He expressed His desire and entrapped energy in time and space. And there was a universe of sparkling stars bunched in galaxies carefully balanced in space. That was a BIG bang.

Now let's go for another spin (and here is where the interesting stuff starts as far as I am concerned; the last was just introductory explanations to warm up the brain cells for actual thought work).

Those who dabble in theology observe that God is 'omnipotent' – there is a lot of energy in being Him. Theologians observe that He is eternal – there is a limitless time factor. They observe that He is omnipresent – He has the space factor covered. They observe that God is omniscient – a knowledge base way beyond our comprehension, so He just might be smart enough to put some things together. They then observe He is personal – He has desires and will. A fundamental quality and mindset of His desires and will is love. From that we can launch into mountains of books that endeavor to comprehend that aspect of God. It is in answer to the property and requirements of love that prompted God to begin expressing His desires for real estate that would serve as substrate to support beings to love, that would return love, and He could watch love one another. He expressed His desires and His desires took shape. He is, after all, all power, all energy, all time, and all space combined. Einstein had used physics to explain his belief in God, and he left it as a hint to us that we could use physics to explain His existence. God can be proven through math. Let's look at one more aspect of this before we stop.

We posit in most physics textbooks that four common dimensions are length, width, height and time; the next dimension of existence is perception.

Perception is a low level function of a mind possessing some level of sentience. Perception is the basic reception and recognition of stimuli. In the first three dimensions of life, length, width, height, which we didn't even comment on particularly, objects in that space are perceived as sets of boundaries of matter, as producers of sound, chemistries realized as tastes and smells. These provide a foundational basis, in conjunction with time, for all of.

Time takes more mental horsepower. We note that in a strict sense 'the present' doesn't really exist. By one functional definition time is an infinitely fine line transitioning the future to the past. Anything beyond this is a perception of sentient intelligence as in measuring or otherwise perceiving two points on a time line. The "present" is a mental construct. "The present" takes different fuzzy boundaries as appropriate to the context under consideration. You are reading this in the present time. Your memory and mental processing have, over time, assembled these marks into letters, words, sentences, ideas – immediate past. The perception of present also includes expectations projected into the near future. You continue reading because you expect more to be there – until the end point of this. But then you expect to move on to another task; the near future boundary of "the present" keeps moving out. Together, the construct of recent history and anticipation of the near future, we perceive and label "the present."

Now, just for fun, playing with your various contexts of the present, as best you can, put that in context of God's mental power and fit that with Jesus' claim, "before Abraham was, I am" (John 8:58). When God so chooses, all of history, indeed, all of time, becomes present tense. Everything that ever was, is. All of your present, future, past, it's here with Him. Nothing is hidden and nothing is unknown. In the mind of God, and the mind of Einstein in trying to explain God, nothing exists unless He wills it. Today try to think awhile about the infinite mind of God and how He knows what you're doing, and where you're going, and how. He is always with you. He says in His words "I am with you even unto the end of this world" (Matthew 28:20). This little book shares some stories and thoughts that I hope help you to come closer to Him. So come back now to present time since Dan wrote that years ago, and in this present work, he is taking on a still larger subject, not just creation and the structure of God, but Dan is taking a systematic look at love, an almost impossibly large subject, with so much tangled up in it. He hopes, as do I, that this book will help you to comprehend "together with all the Lord's holy people, to grasp how wide and long and high and deep is the love of Christ" (Ephesians 3:18). God bless you as you come closer to Him in this season of prayer, introspection and praise.

J. Traveler Pelton LISW-S

18

Chapter 1
Please Read This First

There are very few chapters in this work that can be considered stand-alone. There is an underlying theme that is being built, rather like building a house or a cabinet. It needs to be built in an orderly fashion. You don't start with the roof; you start with a foundation.

I'm setting a foundation here so we are all talking and thinking on the same idea before I add to it. Once you have been through the work in its entirety then going back to particular chapters makes more sense and you will comprehend better what I am trying to say.

Two times in the fourth chapter of John's first letter, John uses the phrase, "God is love." In verse eight he says this, "He who does not love, does not know God, for God is love." "...God is love." I have come to say this is THE prime axiom, the PRIME axiom - a statement self-evident from common experience. From this all else hangs. All aspects of life and learning have something to say about love, how it works, how to (or not to) live it. This phrase is the root, the background, the framework of this study.

Up front I am going to lay down some bullet points which will be further developed later but these assumptions are needed to provide some sort of foundation on which to build our discussion. Our first accepted assumption is simple and I am repeating it just because it is so important:

- <u>God is love.</u> All other assumptions listed hang on that idea. It is the central prime axiom of life.

- The purpose of our existence is to be part of a web of relationships. We were never meant to be alone and we fill a need in God's love as He fills a need in ours.

- "Doctrine" comprises expressions, descriptions of specific aspects of reality. A simple analogy would be this; white light passes through a prism and spreads into colors. The colors are called a spectrum. Looking at the spectrum tells us something about the source of the light. Each color, each line provides another bit of information. Spectrum analysis is used to determine what a tested substance is made of; doctrine does the same thing. It's not God; it's not His Son or Spirit; it's simply a description of what He is like and what we need to be like. Often it describes how relationships work.

- The Bible is our foundational resource for understanding several qualities of love and reality.

  The Bible isn't just a book. It is a library in a single binding. The Bible is comprised of the work of forty authors writing over a span of 1500 years.

- There are observations we can draw from life, living and language that can aid our understanding of concepts raised in the Bible.

- Words are sound symbols into which we pack ideas. Every field of study has its language and nuances of meaning. Learning what God is about certainly has its lingo. At times it may seem a little tedious or even strange. Unless our understanding of the language we use is in close agreement we can wind up just blowing vortexes of heat and smoke and miss what is meant to be understood.

Numerous "systematic theologies" have been written. Many churches and associated entities have a "creed" and/or "statement of beliefs." They all read like a table of contents. Occasionally a text is written that is based on a statement of beliefs and expands the statements to make them more palatable. While they are all carefully, accurately and truthfully written, by very well-meaning scholars; in all such statements and books I have seen they are all fundamentally flawed. That flaw tends to lead to a perspective that misses the essential point of the whole exercise. To merely generate a list of doctrines (with their supporting references) found in the Bible is to miss the point of the doctrines. They are not built on the first three bullet points noted above. As God's love is studied it fans out into an array of doctrines and expressions. Some of those doctrines are going to be addressed in this work but we are going to do our best to cast them as fragment expressions of God's love. They are a piece of a picture. Taken together, they show a wonderful Creator, Redeemer, Lover.

There is another idea that bothers me about "Christian evangelism." We approach people as if they have an understanding of what "salvation" is about and assume it is something desirable they want. Why would I want to be "saved" and live forever? For most people there is an innate desire to live. Even so they may wonder why. To some people sitting on a cloud, playing a harp and singing praises to God sounds like head splitting boredom. I prefer a pipe organ to a harp. It doesn't do clouds. Many Christians look forward to heaven where there is no sickness, old age, death, pain, discouragement and so on. The suffering that we face here won't be there. Well, that's all to the good. But once the pain is gone, what now? The idea of spending eons around the throne praising and adoring God is good, but somehow, there has to be more than that. After a while, won't it sound repetitious and robotic? You can count me out of that one too. Of course there is a place for God to be our god and due adoration presented. On the other hand, He gave us these wonderful brains; He meant us to use them, and singing the Hallelujah chorus every day throughout eternity is not going to keep our interest when there is going to be so much surrounding us. We present a heaven too small to keep our interest. We paint a dim picture. There is more than enough room in heaven's plan to live, learn, play, work, fellowship with fellow humans, other "people" in God's creation, angels, in addition to rightful and central fellowship with God. What about travel and sight-seeing? Even if we revved up our RV and went galaxy hopping, it would take a few million years just to get the "lay of the land" and find a few things we would like to come back to learn about. Believe me when I say all the animators in Hollywood and other places could not dream up much of what we are going to visit.

I hope to provide a sensible, delightful perspective on citizenship in God's kingdom in present and future tense as generally described and experienced from expressions from the past.

In no way is this a definitive study. As a young fellow I climbed a fire observation tower in a state park. The staircase spiraled upward inside the frame of the tower. The entry point was at ground level on the east side of the tower. Each time I came to the east side of the tower I had a different, less limited perspective on the scene around me. When I got above tree level the vista broadened greatly. With this study we enter a tower of knowledge and understanding at ground level. Each time around will build on previous background and see things from new perspective. Even as we walk into eternity this model still fits.

24

Chapter 2
The Root

"God is love." We come back to that seemingly simple statement yet as we take it apart there is some profound stuff there. Let's start a cursory look first and build it up in layers of understanding.

Among the ways God is God is that He precedes and exceeds us in all ways. Paul writes this to the Colossians (1:16, 17): "For by Him all things were created that are in heaven and that are on earth, visible and invisible, whether thrones or dominions or principalities or powers. All things were created through Him and for Him. And He is before all things, and in Him all things consist." Now we add this: "He who built the house has more honor than the house. For every house is built by someone, but He who built all things is God" (Hebrews 3:3, 4.)

The explicit thought to be seen here is that before some point in the past there was nothing - no people, no earth, not even any stars or galaxies. Nothing. That is, nothing but God. So He certainly precedes us. To be able to build everything in reality He certainly exceeds us in ability to design and create.

Say we look at an object before us and say, "That tree is a blue spruce." We have said the object is a tree. We imply it is alive. It is standing. If we know a bit more about trees we know it is classed as soft wood, it is an evergreen, it has needles (not leaves) and has a bluish hue in its coloration. These are all aspects of "it is." When we say "God is love" we link a key descriptive attribute to God. Love becomes an adjective.

So what *is* this "love" thing? Oh, wow! That question has filled libraries. We will try to boil it down to something manageable here but the rest of our consideration will keep adding, filling in, shading in nuances to God's love.

It makes perfect sense to look in a dictionary to find the meaning of a word when you begin a project like this. At the end of this chapter is one of the best efforts at definition by a dictionary and thesaurus I have found. But for the most part it misses God's love so thoroughly I felt it was best tucked away as optional reading. So what is our working definition of love for the purpose of this study?

The essence of love is in relationships of intelligent minds. Each chapter of this work looks at an aspect of such relationships. As we look into our relationships we desire - even crave - being with family and friends, doing things together be it projects/work, travel, games, or just chatter. We have traditions like Christmas gift exchanges, birthday parties, other anniversaries of numerous kinds, holidays... We look out for one another in caring ways. If all this should go away, we become lonely - even ill. One reason for solitary confinement in prison is to prevent possible treachery against other inmates but solitary confinement is also devastating to the one in isolation.

Now let's lay some observations side by side. We noted that *everything* was at some point brought into existence. So by extension, at some point there was nothing - but there was Some One - God. Then we also noted God is love. It is their nature (we'll look into the plural pronoun shortly) to love. Our love of relationship and fellowship is reminiscent of theirs. We can kind of feel for God as being in a form of solitary confinement. They decided to do something about it. So after some deliberation and design... Well, that's the next chapter.

>

I promised you the definitions I had found earlier. Here they are, in no particular order.

Since words are containers for ideas let's start with some summaries found in the Merriam-Webster Online dictionary - formatting adapted for this book. For the moment just glance down the dictionary and thesaurus entries. Note that an important, well-worn word gathers a lot of nuances.

"Definition of love

*1 a (1) : strong affection for another arising out of kinship or personal ties, maternal love for a child (2) : attraction based on sexual desire : affection and tenderness felt by lovers. Ex. After all these years, they are still very much in love. (3) : affection based on admiration, benevolence, or common interests, ex. love for his old schoolmates

>b : an assurance of affection Ex. give her my love

*2: warm **attachment**, enthusiasm, or devotion. Ex.

love of the sea

*3a : the object of attachment, devotion, or admiration

Ex. baseball was his first love

>b (1) : a beloved person : <u>darling</u> —often used as a term of endearment (2) British—used as an informal term of address

*4a : unselfish loyal and benevolent (see <u>benevolent</u> 1a) concern for the good of another: such as (1) : the fatherly concern of God for humankind (2) : brotherly concern for others

> b : a person's adoration of God

*5: a god (such as Cupid or Eros) or <u>personification</u> of love

*6: an <u>amorous</u> episode : <u>love affair</u>

*7: the sexual embrace : <u>copulation</u>

*8: a score of zero (as in tennis)

*9 capitalized, Christian Science : <u>god</u>

I promised you the definitions I had found earlier. Here they are, in no particular order.

Since words are containers for ideas let's start with some summaries found in the <u>Merriam-Webster Online dictionary</u> - formatting adapted for this book. For the moment just glance down the dictionary and thesaurus entries. Note that an important, well-worn word gathers a lot of nuances.

"Definition of love

*1 a (1) : strong affection for another arising out of kinship or personal ties, maternal love for a child (2) : attraction based on sexual desire : affection and tenderness felt by lovers. Ex. After all these years, they are still very much in love. (3) : affection based on admiration, **benevolence**, or common interests, ex. love for his old schoolmates
>b : an assurance of affection Ex. give her my love

*2: warm **attachment**, enthusiasm, or devotion. Ex. love of the sea

*3a : the object of attachment, devotion, or admiration

Ex. baseball was his first love

>b (1) : a beloved person : darling —often used as a term of endearment (2) British—used as an informal term of address
*4a : unselfish loyal and benevolent (see benevolent 1a) concern for the good of another: such as (1) : the fatherly

29

concern of God for humankind (2) : brotherly concern for others

> b : a person's adoration of God

*5: a god (such as Cupid or Eros) or personification of love

*6: an amorous episode : love affair

*7: the sexual embrace : copulation

*8: a score of zero (as in tennis)

*9 capitalized, Christian Science : god

An online thesaurus I consulted collects related words:

*Synonyms and Antonyms of love

>1a feeling of strong or constant regard for and dedication to someone; Ex. Her love for her children was truly selfless.

>Synonyms of love

affection, attachment, devotedness, devotion, fondness, passion

>Words Related to love

appetite, fancy, favor, like, liking, partiality, preference, r elish, taste, craving, crush, desire, infatuation, longing, lu st, yearning, ardor, eagerness, enthusiasm, fervor, zeal, a ppreciation, esteem, estimation, regard, respect, allegianc e, faithfulness, fealty, fidelity, loyalty, steadfastness

>Near Antonyms of love

animosity, antagonism, antipathy, aversion, disfavor, disl
ike, enmity, hostility,
abhorrence, disgust, repugnance, repulsion, revulsion
>Antonyms of love

abomination, hate, hatred, loathing, rancor
*2a person with whom one is in love

She is the love of my life!

>Synonyms of love

beloved, darling, dear, flame, honey, squeeze [slang], sw
eet, sweetheart, sweetie,truelove
>Words Related to love

beau, boy, boyfriend, fellow, man, swain, gal, girl, girlfri
end, ladylove, lass, amour, lover, paramour, date,escort, s
teady, admirer, gallant, suitor, wooer, groom, husband, br
ide, wife, fiancé, intended, crush, heartthrob
*3 positive regard for something

a love of chocolate, which I will pay anything to indulge

>Synonyms of love

appetite, fancy, favor, fondness, like, liking, love
affair, partiality, preference, relish, shine, taste, use
>Words Related to love

craving, desire, hankering, longing, thirst, yen, enthusias
m, gusto, interest, passion,
bias, prejudice, bent, inclination, leaning, propensity, ten
dency, tooth, palate, weakness
>Near Antonyms of love

apathy, disinclination, indifference, unconcern
>Antonyms of love

aversion, disfavor, disgust, dislike, distaste, hatred, loathing, mislike

*4a brief romantic relationship

He refused to discuss past loves.

>Synonyms of love

affair (also affaire), fling, love affair, romance
>Words Related to love

intrigue, liaison, dalliance, hanky-
panky, attachment, infatuation, entanglement, flirtation, idyll (also idyl), passion, calf-love, puppy love

This dictionary and thesaurus did a good job of collecting many ideas associated with "love." At least in the context of relationships between people. However, as you just ploughed through, God doesn't really fit anywhere. I am not entirely certain this is done in error; in the world we live in, with its secularism and control by the opposite of good, why would that evil allow anyone to consider God being part of the definition of love?

Whatsoever, we need to begin sorting through the rubble and shaping the word in ways specific to the God we love, and the why of why He loves us. Let's move on to the next set of ideas.

Chapter 3
Creative Rampage

We built the observation that to be the only being in the universe would have been lonely for God. Somewhere back in time, they decided to do something about that need to share their love. God considered and came to the conclusion that it would be real nice to enjoy a wider field of associations and to share themselves. "God is love." But there was no one around to love. No one with whom to do things. No one with whom to show things. No one to call back saying, "Hey, look at this. I did this and that and look what happened!" No new conversation, discovery, chatter. No one to bump and touch as things are being done together.

So they began to dream, scheme, design. The first thing needed is a place for it all to be - some real estate. They needed a substrate to support everything that came to their minds. Native tribes in the east call God, "He who creates with a thought." And that certainly fits here. They considered all the angles, all the possibilities, and formed a massive plan, a plan large enough for a universe to fit into and have room to grow. I don't have any idea how long that took; after all, they are timeless, so as much time as needed was taken to see that it was created well.

But finally the time had come for the dream to begin taking shape, to become reality. He spoke with intent and the creative rampage was under way. Out of a brilliant blast space began to fill in with galaxies of different sizes and shapes. Galaxies, clusters of stars; stars of different sizes and colors. Sedate stars. Stars rotating rapidly emitting spiraling beams of light. Pairs, even sets, of stars dancing in mutual orbit. Some stars came equipped with satellites orbiting them. Lazy, hazy clouds floated in the space scape. It all formed a scene of beautiful, awesome splendor just as He wanted. We look back on that event now and call it "The Big Bang." Astronomers and physicists look back at the evidence and say it occurred nearly 14 billion years ago. God is eternal. What's a few billion years to Him?

Truly. "By the word of the Lord the heavens were made, And all the host of them by the breath of His mouth. For He spoke, and it was done; He commanded, and it stood fast" Psalm 33:6, 9.

Now He had a place for the next bit of work to go. If you search the word "angel" in the Bible nearly 300 entries appear. Cherub/cherubim appears some 70 times. Ezekiel (chapters 1 and 10) resorts to just trying to describe some "creatures" around the throne of God. Trying to understand his astonished eyewitness in a vision report is pretty entertaining, wheels within wheels and faces on all sides…poor Ezekiel had no words.

Another Old Testament book, Job, talks of the throne room of God. Job had been through a very difficult period in his life. He had raised some serious and challenging questions of God. He was tested like none of the rest of us have been and still remained true to his Maker, but he had questions. God loves His children and He finally comes to address Job. In the course of the address to him, God refers to the establishment of the earth. "Where were you ... When the morning stars sang together, And all the sons of God shouted for joy?" (Job 38:4, 7) There was life in existence before this earth was created. They watched in delighted amazement as God did His work. They will be there for us to meet someday. They can tell us what watching our creation was like.

We are not the only life in the universe. We were not the first life to be created. We will one day have fellowship with the universe. To think we are the only creation of God is possibly the most egotistical, narcissistic idea in the world. Yet let's get back to God and what He was doing.

Let's turn to Genesis one. "In the beginning God created the heavens and the earth. The earth was without form, and void; and darkness was on the face of the deep. And the Spirit of God was hovering over the face of the waters." The first sentence is a general comment - a summary of fact. The second sentence begins to address the earth specifically. This language indicates the planet was here in raw, undeveloped form. It was dark, dank, dull. Then God began to direct His attention to it. It says "the Spirit of God was hovering..." That "hovering" is not in the sense of a helicopter holding its place over a fixed point. It's more like brooding, sitting close, waiting, expecting.

Indeed, something does begin to happen. God began to speak, "'Let there be light'; and there was light. And God saw the light, that it was good; and God divided the light from the darkness. God called the light Day, and the darkness He called Night. So the evening and the morning were the first day" verses 3-5. It wasn't a general light. It took sides. This is evidence of the earth's rotation as the cycle of day and night is noted.

This pattern becomes a template for most of the creation record. God speaks. Something happens. God rates it. Each night and day is numbered. It is noteworthy that God starts the daily period with the quiet part. Then the evening fades into light and the business of the day starts.

I am a somewhat creative person and I have built things: my house, and shelves and a barn. After the building is done, you take a moment, you stand back and look at it, and you smile. Yes, that's what I wanted. It awes me that each day of creation, the Lord stood back, looked it over, checked a few things then smiled. He said "It is good."

Chapter one of Genesis walks through the overall sequence of events in development of this planet. Chapter two is an overview from a different perspective. I would suggest just reading through both chapters right now for a good overview of the creation week.

Up through the first half of day six God is building an environment. He built a set of systems that support life. He provided water systems. The solar gravity along with the moon's pull sloshes water to aid in moving and pumping water through the cycle it would need to keep everything hydrated. Water will get more discussion later. Solar powered plant life provides food for an amazing array other lifeforms. There are so many synergistic systems set up in these first six days. I'll mention a few that astonish me:

Bees. I keep bees. A colony of bees is amazing. There are many tasks to be fulfilled in a hive. In general bees move through performance of tasks by age. A queen provides enough offspring to maintain a hive of 50,000 bees. She sets up the nursery. Young bees care for that. There are wax production and clean up divisions. Ventilation/temperature control/water divisions, evaporation to ripen honey is all balanced. Guard duty goes on daily; field work bringing in nectar, pollen, water for air conditioning, certain materials to make propolis which is a glue/caulking compound to patch holes or perhaps encapsulate a mouse they couldn't haul out, all run without a hitch. For the field work, bees are stunning navigators finding flower fields that may be miles away. Scouts go find flower fields and communicate their location by dancing! They pass out samples. Then workers know how to fuel up, what they are looking for and where to go to bring home the goods.

That's half the story. Those fields of flowers need the bees to move pollen around so they can make seed for their propagation and fruit for other life - like us - to have delicious, nutritious things to eat. Keeping bees is a little like overseeing a city running all by itself. I wonder sometimes if God watches us that way?

Moving closer to home, there are micro life forms on our skin to keep other life forms in their place for our defense and our maintenance. Other micro-life in our gut is essential for part of the digestion process and making necessary nutrients. These bacteria are essential to our survival.

I have kept sheep, goats, alpaca - all members of the "ruminant" group of animals. They all eat grass. Cellulose is a major structural material in grass that is rather tough and difficult to chemically break down. But ruminants process their food through several processing chambers. They eat the grass. After a little pretreatment it comes back up for a second chewing (It's called chewing their cud, and if you watch cows or camelids relax after eating for several hours, you can see the lumps of processed grass come up and be re-chewed, then swallowed and another lump come up their neck as a slight ascending bulge; incredible.). Then the grass passes through "vats" of microbes for fermentation and post processing to provide the nutrients needed by the animal. Neither the microbes nor the animals can live without each other.

Synergistic systems throughout nature are a fascinating study in their own right. Each system set has to be fully functional or it doesn't work at all. Not only do all the functions in the beehive have to work, all the flowers have to be there in their season and throughout the season. The right kind of animal needs the right of microbes to process the right kind of grass. Any missing link disables the whole system.

And what of the property of life itself? The design and function within each cell is bewildering to understand. The very structure of the cell along with its membranes, nucleus, mitochondria and organelles must be constantly maintained by the processes of life or it soon disintegrates. Then to maintain the existence of the life form it must replicate itself. That is another outstanding feat of design. It is well established that life can only be handed down from life. Louis Pasteur established spontaneous generation of life, life coming into existence from nothing, was not a demonstrable hypothesis. Every grocery store with its canning, freezing, bottling is demonstration of this. Emergency rations are available with a 25 year shelf life. Even then it's not that the sealed food spoils but eventually the complex compounds break down.

As you read the accounts of the creation of life on days three, five and six you notice that each life form was to reproduce "according the their kinds." And that is what we see - without exception.

Not only is the whole of creation highly functional - it is beautiful in so many ways. As our curiosity probes and discovers how things work it makes more and more sense to appreciate the work of the Designer. Often we just look out, we look down, we look up, we look around, at times we just stand in awe gawking that the beauty of color, form and even function.

Ten times God says something like "let there be..." and it happens just as He says. Then there is a change in the pattern. He says, "Let Us make..." (verse 26). "'Let Us make man in Our image, according to Our likeness; let them have dominion...'" "So God created man in His own image; in the image of God He created him; male and female He created them" (verse 27). "In the day that God created man, He made him in the likeness of God. He created them male and female, and blessed them and called them Mankind in the day they were created" (Genesis 5:1, 2). "Therefore a man shall leave his father and mother and be joined to his wife, and they shall become one flesh" Genesis 2:24. (We will use this paragraph as a reference paragraph and refer back to it as "the reference paragraph.")

I have been warned that it is audacious and highly improper to commit "anthropomorphism." What a lovely long word! It means ascribing, giving to God human properties and attributes. He is so grand, so above and beyond us it is grossly demeaning to try to reduce Him to our terms. Well, I have the audacity to turn the tables. He says He made us, at least in some regards, like Him! So there are attributes He and us must have in common. Naming those similarities isn't giving God human attributes; it's recognizing His attributes in us! There are attributes we have that are different yet recognizably similar. And we need to be rightfully aware of attributes we do not, can not and will never have in common with Him. It is well we come to appreciate each zone of attributes. And again, we'll get into some of that.

So now let's look at that "Let Us make..." thing a little bit. Down in verse seven of Genesis chapter two we read: "And the Lord God formed man of the dust of the ground, and breathed into his nostrils the breath of life; and man became a living being." This is a summary of how He did it. There's more detail here about how He did it than was given in the general report recorded in chapter one. Let's try to visualize how this may have happened. Imagine this, if you will.

First, review the events of the third day. God drew land up from the water. He then set vast areas and varieties of plants. However, in my mind's eye I see that He left a mucky pool - probably surrounded by cattails and reeds. He had plans for that spot. Now in a later part of day six it says He "formed man of the dust of the ground." It wasn't dry dust. We aren't dry; scientists say the average adult is 60% water. Wet dust would be muck, a combination of organic materials and minerals and it wouldn't hold together, so I am suspicioning this was clay such as is used by potters or artist to sculpt something. The only way to make something in clay is to get into it. Picture God with a bit of a grin on His face stepping into this pool of mucky clay, stooping down and beginning to work up a shape. It begins to look a bit familiar. Three times in that reference paragraph we see that there is a likeness to God. It is said God is spirit. Some people assume a "spirit" is a shapeless, ethereal, non-material essence and thus our likeness to God is in ways other than personal appearance. Perhaps there are grounds to question that assumption that God has no physical attributes. Your likeness can be recognized in a photograph. Is the likeness you? Certainly not. There are some dimensions missing like depth, life, warmth, thought. So there are recognizable attributes of God in us. Those attributes of God in us are closer than the photograph is to you. We see God finish the sculpting. He sits back. Looks over His handiwork. Our amazement deepens as He leans over on all fours and "breathes into his nostrils the breath of life." We see something like this in CPR but I suggest we look at the scene and think again. This is the posture of a kiss! We watch as the color of that sculpture changes slightly. It begins to move. Indeed, he rises to his feet. God and man greet each other. They walk out of that muck pool into a beautiful expanse. With a kiss God lights the fire of life in this special, handmade, one of a kind creature. When God said, "Let Us make..." He did just that. This was not a here-is-what-I-want-and-there-it-is project. We see special, individual, personalized design and effort. We see special relationship, even love written all over this part of the creative project.

He isn't done yet. "It is not good that man should be alone; I will make him a helper comparable to him," Genesis 2:18. Adam didn't even know yet that he had a problem. God could have just told him he wasn't complete, but He knew it would be a more lasting lesson if He allowed Adam to come to the conclusion himself, so God gave him his first job. God invites the animals to come by and meet this new part of creation - Adam, their new leader. As they come by Adam names them. It doesn't take long for him to realize they all come by twos. While each pair are alike there is also a difference, color, size, physical attributes. Adam begins to look for something like himself and there just isn't. He looks up at God and he begins to feel funny, sort of dizzy and weak and fatigued so he lays down and falls into a deep sleep- the first anesthesia. God performs the first surgery, removes a rib and returns to that muck pool. He sticks that rib into the muck and forms around it a similar but different sculpture. With a kiss this one too rises to her feet and they exchange greetings. She is stunning absolutely a ten, Miss Universe herself! She walks with Him out of the pool into the beautiful expanse. God and she don't get far. Adam is just waking up. His eyes land on this new creature. Oh, my! Missus Adam is a wonder to behold! He has his match - his completion, not from his head to lord it over her; not from his feet to be stepped on, but from his side, to walk alongside as an equal. Adam has his consort, his companion, his mate, his one of a kind forever love.

Now there is something else we need to see in that "Let Us make..." As we read Genesis 1:26 and 27 look for a peculiar mix of singular and plural choice of words. "God" and "man" are singular form yet they are also addressed with plural pronouns. The plurality of man is further called out as "male and female." We'll later study the "us" of God. Right now we are looking at man.

"Then God said, 'Let Us make man in Our image, according to Our likeness...' So God created man in His own image; in the image of God He created him; male and female He created them."

This plural oneness is presented in additional terms in Genesis 2:24, "Therefore a man shall leave his father and mother and be joined to his wife, and they shall become one flesh." The mind and bodies of men and women work differently in a way that is complementary and completing. When you plug a lamp into the wall receptacle you complete the circuit. That connection is complementary and completing. There is known to be a strong emotional bonding associated with sexual intercourse that is established with hormonal and neurological ties. When exercised in the context of a love bound covenant an amazing entity is fostered which often expands as children join them. Discussion of "microchimerism," particularly in the sense of finding male DNA (cells with the x-y sex chromosomes) in female brains, is beginning to appear in biological research. The question is being asked if DNA sharing that happens during reproduction may be an aspect of a couple indeed becoming "one flesh."

As we read the prayer of Jesus recorded in John 17 we discover another aspect of human oneness. He was/is looking forward to all of humanity being a unity (verses 20-23). I cannot imagine what this is about; however it is a desired state of being that somehow preserves our individual personalities, yet integrates all levels of our relationships into a single human entity that is even united with God in a mystical joining of Church and Him. We become His bride, the Bride of Christ. Perhaps an illustration can be found when we assemble large music ensembles as in large choirs and orchestras. I have performed in such a setting. It is wonderful, unforgettable, and leaves me with a desire to do it all again, the rehearsals, the practice, the dress up and get up in front and let the voices fly to the heavens together.

Imagine a Venn diagram; three circles, overlapping in such a way that the middle section is overlaid. (There is one on the back cover.) Each circle is representing a member of the Godhead, Father, Son and Holy Spirit. In your mind, imagine you see exclusive areas, restricted inclusions, and an area of universal inclusion. There is an area exclusive to each member. Each is an individual but each overlaps into a family unit that together is called One God. This One God has three parts. The three parts have different responsibilities in the universe, but all are God. There is much they share in common likeness. We noted He precedes and exceeds us in all things. This creative rampage that ended up with us coming into existence demonstrates the power of God to plan, execute and maintain us. We cannot be eternal as in having no beginning. We had a beginning, a definite point at which we became. God didn't, He has always been, an idea that is hard to wrap our finite minds around.

At this point in creation our reach into eternity future is conditional and even then it will be dependent where His is independent. His love blankets the universe where ours is local. We are a model of what God is; could we say that as His family is the creative redemptive living source in the universe, we were made in an image of Him so He could be more understood by the universe?

There is a common inclusive area in our Venn diagram where all the members overlap. Love is a common need and quality. Our social nature comes from love. (Our social relationship with God tends to be called "worship.") We are creative. We design and shape our homes, the arts, music, parks and gardens, infrastructures, mechanisms, all for mutual benefit. We even create in our image - our children. Through Jesus God even has a human element.

I have an exclusive, personal relationship with God. So do you. Yet together we have a common fellowship with Him.

There are ways I am me and exclusive of you. I am male. You may not be. I am a technician with some general knowledge of machines, electrons, carpentry. I lift the hood of a car and recognize numerous parts and systems. Someone else opens the hood and sees a darkish mass of... of whatever. I get baffled by people (especially children), money and many other things. This is why we trade and share the accomplishment of projects.

In the 'Me and Others' common area there are exclusives. I have one wife. A set of exclusives comes with that. Husbands, wives, children, families even with their exclusives are common to being human. My association with our children changes as they grow. My exclusives with them become smaller as they grow toward more general relationships. Through eternity they will be exclusively our children - our offspring. There are special things especially close friends share and understand. There are many things in common with being human and being in the web of relationships.

<u>End of Chapter notes</u>

<u>More information on the DNA bonding can be found here.</u>

https://www.psychologicalscience.org/news/releases/a-48-hour-sexual-afterglow-helps-to-bond-partners-over-time.html

http://www.familylife.com/articles/topics/parenting/challenges/sexual-purity/hooked-the-bonding-power-of-sex
http://www.collective-evolution.com/2014/03/18/this-study-will-make-you-think-twice-about-who-you-are-getting-into-bed-with/

Chapter 4
Another Way God is Love is as Our Provider.

In the development of our understanding that God is love, we saw that He desired a broadened field of relationships; love begets love. Love is creative and it has to enlarge its borders and grow and multiply. He had to make some provisions to be able to spread out, to stretch across the empty spaces and fill them. He needed a place for "people" (a variety of intelligent minds and cultures) to live. So He made some real estate - in our small comprehension we call it the "universe." He populated it with a variety of intelligent beings and even some helpful creatures. To this point we are considering this "provision" idea as a near synonym for "creation." But there is an aspect of provision that basic creation doesn't quite cover. We are going to take another pass over Genesis one and two from a little different angle - from another level of the fire tower, if you please.

"And God said, 'See, I have given you every herb that yields seed which is on the face of all the earth, and every tree whose fruit yields seed; to you it shall be for food. Also, to every beast of the earth, to every bird of the air, and to everything that creeps on the earth, in which there is life, I have given every green herb for food.'" Genesis 1:29, 30. God provided food composed of greens, seeds, and fruit for man and all the animals.

"...fill the earth and subdue it..." Gen 1:28. "The Lord God planted a garden eastward in Eden, and there He put the man whom He had formed" "Then the Lord God took the man and put him in the garden of Eden to tend and keep it" Gen 2:8, 15. God provided Adam something to do. Some of the mechanisms of Earth worked differently then. God said they were to "subdue it."

The on-line Merriam-Webster Dictionary has these entries under "subdue:"

1: to conquer and bring into subjection : vanquish
2: to bring under control especially by an exertion of the will : to curb as in subdued my foolish fears
3: to bring (land) under cultivation
4: to reduce the intensity or degree of : tone down

The first dictionary entry is of little interest here as God was handing Adam dominion. There was no conquering needed, no fight, no battle, nothing to overrun or vanquish as it was simply given to him. As created the world was already gentle so dictionary entry four isn't where we are going; there was nothing to tone down. With some tweaking lines two and three have interest to us.

One way we resemble God is in creativity. We can't make something from nothing. We *can* dream of things and shape what is around us to bring ideas to reality.

Curiosity is another amazing quality we share with God. The question mark is the hallmark of curiosity. The best learning and education is found beyond questions.

I remember way back when I was a little tyke of maybe four. My Dad had found an aviation gyroscope like would be used in an artificial horizon. It was a small motor spinning a heavy wheel at high speed. There was an almost silent whoosh as it ran. He had me touch the wheel with a stick. It promptly smelled of smoke and blackened. Then he said, "Here. But don't touch the wheel." As I took hold of it I nearly dropped it. When you lift a stick it just - well it just lifts. But this thing Dad had brought! I went to tilt it up to get a closer look and it pulled forcefully to the right. My own surprise reflex had me struggling to not drop this thing. Dad has long since forgotten that incident but look at my memory of it. It sparked questions in my mind and I have never stopped asking questions. In time I learned about precession which made that spinning wheel act so strange and be so useful to navigation. I learned more about the friction that made that stick smoke. I was fascinated with electricity and magnetism which made the motor work. I learned of tubes and transistors to control electricity in various ways. I learned of Bernoulli's principle as it applies to birds and airplanes flying. Yes, school refined my understanding of such things but my own curiosity drove me to exhaust the technical sections of the library, and poke, prod, play, and experiment with the world around me. Following questions funded much of the knowledge and wisdom for my career. It made me a technician and inventor, a writer and theologian forever in training.

Different minds work differently. Some find beauty and delight in placing flowers in beautiful arrangements. Some are delighted with the way processes and numbers make profit in business. Some are enchanted with sounds of music. Everyone has their own flavor of curiosity and what they find delightful. But pursuit of curiosity is behind the best and most intuitive learning.

I am a technician by nature. My career was in fixing things and working with the development of new systems. Accordingly here are some levels of thought to consider in our study of Love and God. Can it be our curiosity is why God gave us free choice? Is the sameness of everything working perfectly one of the reasons He allowed us the ability to be unpredictable?

A scientist is one who has a deep curiosity - "How does that work?" "What happens if we do this?" "Oh, wow! Look at what happened!"

An engineer looks at what the scientist discovered and says, "We can make that do this for us. Let's figure out how to make it do just what we want." He figures out the functions, systems, stresses, shapes, materials that need to be put together.

Then he hands descriptions to machinists, circuit board designers, programmers - technical staff who begin to turn a dream, an idea, into reality. All these parts come to a place where assembly technicians put it all together.

The engineer gives a test plan to the engineering technicians who gently start the system up and see if it meets the needs of the test plan and the operating specifications the engineer intended.

God provided all these wonderful traits of thought, all of them based on free choice.

Adam probably did not have to work with a development staff as we described. He was primarily a gardener and keeper of a zoo without fences or hard boundaries. Even that was very different from what it is now. There was no limit to his life so he didn't have to get it done by the first of the month or before retirement. If he wanted a meadow here, an orchard there, a scented herb bed along that ridge he got it done to his liking. If he wanted a hole dug, he called a badger over and said right here, about this wide, this deep - and his friend dug him a hole. The elephant lifted the tree and held it in place as he patted the dirt around the roots. In my mind's fancy, I can see he and his animal friends and his wife arranging different sections of Eden, pruning back vines, setting up rose trellis's, picking a pear here to eat as a snack while contemplating red poppies here or yellow tulips? A lilac bush here, forsythia there, maybe a pile of gold with some diamonds stuck to it would be sparkly and shiny and pretty to use as a seat. Imagine God as teacher, letting Adam see he needed to understand what the light and water needs were for each and shape their place appropriately. Adam was a scientist seeing how things worked. He did engineering fitting things together. He was a technician getting it done. If it took 600 years for this or 250 for that - it was given no thought. If he found a beautiful stone he could mount it in a pendant for his wife. Since jewels didn't have monetary value, he could take a handful of emeralds and a few rubies and make a pretty crystal shaded window as a surprise for Eve. Did they plant trees and bushes in a square and let them all grow together to make a house? They were able to shape and manage (subdue) Eden to their liking. There was no greed, no plunder, no harm done.

Genesis says Adam had dominion over the life of earth. To a very limited degree we still do. Some creatures (water buffalo, oxen, horses, mules) serve as tractors to help with heavy work. Bees make honey, pollinate many of our crops, beeswax has a variety of uses. Hair of various animals can be made into an assortment of beautiful and useful articles. To some extent we can communicate with animals. I am aware of contentment or concern as I watch and listen to my bees, chickens, alpaca or cats. Some can even read what I am about and seem to sit there studying me. They sometimes give me their opinions - the kittens need something, the dog has noticed something unusual. When we bring in hay from the field, the alpaca have to come inspect it and hum their pleasure at the nice pile going into the hay barn. There is a high degree of communication between a shepherd and his dog or a horse and rider - each with its' own vocabulary. Some animals are around us just for companionship. In the time near Adam's creation all of nature was companionable and cooperative. While there was much time for play, if Adam wanted to plant a walnut tree right there a squirrel did it. If Adam wanted a guided tour of a reef a dolphin was delighted to take him through. He could even be tickled by an octopus. The Bible doesn't take the space to tell of such things. We see remnants of some of it today in the closeness we feel to our pets. As we look at cues in upcoming history we will note decline and breakdown in our association with nature.

It is valuable for us to paint some kind of picture of Adam's life and activity. He was active, involved, content. To look way forward for a moment, we are on a detour in a disrupted world. From this look at Adam's time in the garden we can find clues to the potential of life when we get off this detour - when we realize our salvation. There are other passages in the Bible that give us more clues as to what the ideal life ought to be for us.

There is another way we resemble God. He said to Adam (remember this is plural - not just him), "Be fruitful and multiply" Genesis 1:28. They were to have children. God made us in His likeness. They, too, are in our likeness. They grow up to be nearly our peers. Then the children have children. Thus the web of relationships grows. Remember - God is love. He wanted - needed - a web of relationships where that love could expand and flourish. And so do we. Indeed, the purpose of our existence is to be part of a web of relationships. He provided for an expanding web of relationships. Once again, we were not meant to be alone.

Another thing we see is people getting together to do things. We play games together. We go places together. We plan large projects to work on together. Different minds work differently. In planning to do something or solve a problem we often "group think" to find an answer. Consider the many types of meetings we find ourselves in. They are all part of our relational nature.

There is one more day of creation we haven't mentioned yet - the seventh day. Here is record of that day: "Thus the heavens and the earth, and all the host of them, were finished. And on the seventh day God ended His work which He had done, and He rested on the seventh day from all His work which He had done. Then God blessed the seventh day and sanctified it, because in it He rested from all His work which God had created and made" Genesis 2:1-3. God later personally etched this statement in stone: "Remember the Sabbath day, to keep it holy. Six days you shall labor and do all your work, but the seventh day is the Sabbath of the Lord your God. In it you shall do no work: you, nor your son, nor your daughter, nor your male servant, nor your female servant, nor your cattle, nor your stranger who is within your gates. For in six days the Lord made the heavens and the earth, the sea, and all that is in them, and rested the seventh day. Therefore the Lord blessed the Sabbath day and hallowed it" Exodus 20:8-11.

This day was "blessed" - given special honor and recognition. It was "sanctified," "hallowed" - set aside for special, holy purpose.

Let's reference "God is love" again. Everything was brought into existence to provide a field of love. Here is a day to put away the tools and the work. So now what? Think "date," time to spend with a loved one. When God is our god He is the Love of our life. The Sabbath, then, becomes a weekly date with the Love of our life. God spread His love around so we can love each other. So now friends and family become part of this "date." So this day, then, embodies the whole purpose of creation. God provided time to focus on love and fellowship - relationships. A day looked forward to with anticipation.

"The Lord God planted a garden eastward in Eden, and there He put the man whom He had formed. And out of the ground the Lord God made every tree grow that is pleasant to the sight and good for food. The tree of life was also in the midst of the garden, and the tree of the knowledge of good and evil...

"Then the Lord God took the man and put him in the garden of Eden to tend and keep it. And the Lord God commanded the man, saying, 'Of every tree of the garden you may freely eat; but of the tree of the knowledge of good and evil you shall not eat, for in the day that you eat of it you shall surely die'" Genesis 2:8, 9, 15-17.

As wonderful as it all was there was a place of special comfort and arrangement - a garden. This is where the term "Garden of Eden" comes from. There were many trees in the garden that provided fruit and nuts free for the taking. There were two special trees - the "tree of life" and "the tree of the knowledge of good and evil." Of all the trees they were free to eat - except. Except one tree was pointed out as to be left alone on pain of death - whatever that was. The way He spoke of it "evil" and "death" didn't sound good. In all the garden, indeed in all the world everything was open and available to Adam. This one exception provided one more thing. That one thing was necessary to be fully the voluntary love God found essential and valuable - choice. One who does not provide for or allow choice is a tyrant, a dictator, a totalitarian ruler. God wants none of that. As you look back over all that has been provided it is loaded with choices and opportunities to do an amazing array of things. God even provided choice to go wrong. He made us unpredictable. He wants someone who could understand a little more about Him, about creativity, about curiosity, about family ties.

A powerful instruction in computer programming code is: "if( ), then( ), else( )." If(you eat of the tree of the knowledge of good and evil), then(you die), else(life goes on). The preferred option is don't eat of that tree and life goes on, and on and on... -

Chapter 5
Option Taken, Part One

Picture this: There are two containers in front of me. In each container is a honey colored liquid. Each is labeled with a cost per quart. One label is marked "detergent." The other label is marked "motor oil." I dip a finger in the oil and feel it. It's smooth and slippery. I go to the sink and rinse it off. Uh-oh. Not only does it not come off it smears all over and makes a mess! Hesitantly I examine the detergent. It too is smooth and slippery - or is the slippery still the oil? I try the sink again. Lo and behold the soap rinses off and takes the oil with it! I like that! Its cost is a bit less than the oil and it simply cleans up a mess in water. It's slippery. It's a bit cheaper. It's neater. The book says to use motor oil in the engine. But I like the detergent better. Besides I've heard there is detergent in oil. So detergent it is. A gallon goes right in there.

I get in the car and start for town. Something sounds different. Something doesn't smell right. Then with a lurch the car... the car just stops.

The car gets towed to a mechanic. As he walks to the car he notices an odd smell. He lifts the hood. He looks in amazement. There is froth all over. He looks at me and asks, "What is this?!"

"I don't know. I just changed the oil."

"You changed it to what?"

"Duhh-h-h."

"Well whatever. That'll cost you a new engine."

"But... But."

"Let me replace it or you can junk the whole thing."

I made some choices. I knew better. I did it my way. Oh, boy did it cost me! (And lest you think I am short of a working hamster in the old brain wheel, this was an illustration only. I really didn't do it.)

Is the car care manual crude and demanding for not letting me run what I wanted in the engine? Or might the engineer and manufacturer know something about how it works best?

This is the essence of what we will study next - indeed, the rest of the Bible could be considered a lesson in soap and oil.

Before we take up the events of Genesis 3 we need to go extraterrestrial and pick up another thread of events. In the chapter "Creative Rampage" we noted evidence angels had been created before work on this Earth commenced. There are some passages that tell of one angel in particular that is key to making a lot of history. We will open his story by looking at a passage in the book of Ezekiel, chapter 28.

It is of interest to take a brief look at the first verses of the chapter. Note that it is addressed "to the prince of Tyre." A prince is the son of a king. The sense of the original language here is not father/son but close mentor/disciple. You can see what is on the prince's mind:

"Son of man, say to the prince of Tyre, 'Thus says the Lord God: "Because your heart is lifted up, And you say, 'I am a god, I sit in the seat of gods, In the midst of the seas,' Yet you are a man, and not a god, Though you set your heart as the heart of a god. (Behold, you are wiser than Daniel! There is no secret that can be hidden from you! With your wisdom and your understanding You have gained riches for yourself, And gathered gold and silver into your treasuries; By your great wisdom in trade you have increased your riches, And your heart is lifted up because of your riches)," Ezekiel 28:2-5.

God follows up with these observations:

"Because you have set your heart as the heart of a god, Behold, therefore, I will bring strangers against you, The most terrible of the nations; And they shall draw their swords against the beauty of your wisdom, And defile your splendor. They shall throw you down into the Pit, And you shall die the death of the slain In the midst of the seas" Ezekiel 28: 6-8.

You can hear the kings thinking in the princes thoughts. He was one of great ability. He held wealth, wisdom, knowledge and power. He thought highly of himself even as a god worthy of highest honors. Yet his esteem, his honor, his power would be broken and his humanity would be made known.

In verse 11 Ezekiel is asked to "take up a lamentation for the king of Tyre." A lament is a passionate expression of grief, not just a sad story, but a deeply felt wail of sorrow. God had something to weep about and He wanted us to know about it, and learn the why of it. God here begins to explain the origin of evil in our world. Evil wasn't created here on earth, to the contrary, the earth and our first parents were good, perfect. God wants us to know what happened.

"You were the seal of perfection, Full of wisdom and perfect in beauty. You were in Eden, the garden of God; Every precious stone was your covering: The sardius, topaz, and diamond, Beryl, onyx, and jasper, Sapphire, turquoise, and emerald with gold. The workmanship of your timbrels and pipes was prepared for you on the day you were created. You were the anointed cherub who covers; I established you; You were on the holy mountain of God; You walked back and forth in the midst of fiery stones. You were perfect in your ways from the day you were created..."

This was one awesome personage. He was surrounded with opulent, brilliant splendor. He was in the presence of God. His home address was a place we call heaven;

where God resides. He was in Eden, he saw the creation happen; he watched it unfold. He wasn't born - he was created. Except of Adam (they were created), people are born. The passage twice refers to this being's creation. He was the epitome of creative perfection. Until...

"You were perfect in your ways from the day you were created, Till iniquity was found in you. By the abundance of your trading you became filled with violence within, and you sinned;"

We do well to carefully digest this passage. The prince was created perfect and he was given free will, just as we were given. He was not created to fail or turn or be a yes man. Having said that there were risk factors.

One risk factor was his position. While it was a high position, even by God's throne, there were parameters fitting to his station. If you think of him as a sort of Prime Minister, he was high up in government in heaven, in fact, the right hand man to God. He brought messages from God. He was in charge of communications.

Another risk factor was choice; he had free choice.

We break here for some word study.[1] We need to understand what happened to make this perfect being

---

[1] Biblical word studies, unless otherwise, noted are based on the Strong's Exhaustive Concordance of the Bible. Often "iniquity" and "sin" are used rather interchangeably. Here there is a distinction worth noting.

change so much. It is unexpected for something so perfect to fall so far. A look at word meanings can help us ferret out what happened. God uses the word iniquity as something odd found within the prince. What is iniquity? What is sin? What is the difference, if there is one? Put up a sticky note here. We are going to look at another passage then come back to this word study.

We turn to Isaiah 14. In verse four we "take up this proverb against the king of Babylon..." With verse 12 the rant gets personal and specific.

"How you are fallen from heaven,
O Lucifer, son of the morning!
How you are cut down to the ground,
You who weakened the nations!
For you have said in your heart:
'I will ascend into heaven,
I will exalt my throne above the stars of God;
I will also sit on the mount of the congregation
On the farthest sides of the north;
I will ascend above the heights of the clouds,
I will be like the Most High.'
Yet you shall be brought down to Sheol,
To the lowest depths of the Pit."

First note that the "king of Tyre" was "on the holy mountain of God" - at the very throne of God. The "king of Babylon" has "fallen from heaven." Here we hear the name of this king – Lucifer. We hear what is on this mind in his "I will..." campaign. The king and Tyre and the king of Babylon is the same personage. Indeed, this king, Lucifer, is the functional ruler behind many a kingdom and nation as we saw the thinking of the "prince of Tyre" tracking the thinking of the "king of Tyre."

With this background we return to the word study.

In Ezekiel 28:15 we see the word "iniquity." In this context it tends to carry the idea - to distort, to discolor, to warp. In the setting we are looking at it might look something like this: Lucifer was a key point of contact between God and the hosts of His kingdom. Lucifer would often convey communication from God. Those communications would generally be prefaced with, "God says..." or "He would like..." But at some point a slight change might be heard. "We say..." "We would like..." Lucifer liked the "inclusive" language - including himself with God. In doing this he discolored the message. We was re-framing himself as God. When this re-framing was called to his attention he said something like "whatever" and continued. At this point it became sin (vs 16) - willful disregard of right and correction.

James, in the New Testament, expresses this progression: "Let no one say when he is tempted, 'I am tempted by God'; for God cannot be tempted by evil, nor does He Himself tempt anyone. But each one is tempted when he is drawn away by his own desires and enticed. Then, when desire has conceived, it gives birth to sin; and sin, when it is full-grown, brings forth death" James 1:13-15. Though Lucifer was given all he could handle there was something else he wanted , a deep desire. When it was pointed out that his desire was inappropriate and unattainable he continued to act the same. That sort of stubborn denial after correction of a thinking error results in demise.

Let's use driving a car as a model. When driving down a straight road there are various pressures that lean the car in various ways; side winds, bumps, tilts in the road surface. These nudge us off the road , like iniquities nudge our mind away from God. A little negative correction, slight turn back to center, keeps us on the road. If we become distracted, or, say, we like the berm better than the pavement we wreck , that is, we sin. Lucifer did it big time.

Tensions rose. "And war broke out in heaven: Michael and his angels fought with the dragon; and the dragon and his angels fought, but they did not prevail, nor was a place found for them in heaven any longer. So the great dragon was cast out, that serpent of old, called the Devil and Satan, who deceives the whole world; he was cast to the earth, and his angels were cast out with him" Revelation 12:7-9. Even his name changed. He was Lucifer - "son of the morning." Now he is Satan - "adversary," even likened to a raging dragon. Rather than trading in truth and honor he trades in deception for by deception he engages others in his service in ways and to ends that would be undesirable if the outcome were known.

And, we see what happened. The devil invented himself and he wanted to strike back at the heart of God. One who has been so high wants revenge. He looked around the universe and what did he see? The newest jewel in God's family, the baby, the darling of everyone. It's time move to Genesis three.

"Now the serpent was more cunning than any beast of the field which the Lord God had made. And he said to the woman..." Genesis 3:1.

Chapter 6
Option Taken , Part Two

"Now the serpent was more cunning than any beast of the field which the Lord God had made. And he said to the woman, "Has God indeed said, 'You shall not eat of every tree of the garden?'

And the woman said to the serpent, 'We may eat the fruit of the trees of the garden; but of the fruit of the tree which is in the midst of the garden, God has said, 'You shall not eat it, nor shall you touch it, lest you die.'

Then the serpent said to the woman, 'You will not surely die. For God knows that in the day you eat of it your eyes will be opened, and you will be like God, knowing good and evil' " (Genesis 3:1-5).

The serpent is described as "cunning." It was eye catching, to say the least. It was the instrument chosen to disarm Adam. Every animal he had seen thus far was friendly and trustworthy and good. Adam would have seen this animal as the latest in a world of wonders.

A well-chosen question can raise another question. Good teachers use this technique to draw out answers from students, to train them to think and not parrot back replies. In Eve's mind, looking at the first talking animal she'd ever seen, who was saying something that appeared to be working for him, came the thought, "Why not?" Look back how Eve answered the snake, the dragon in the tree. Careful consideration of her answer already may contain a deflection from the rules given. She addressed the tree in a general way as the "one in the midst of the garden" rather than "this one." To this day, if we are having a discussion and it sounds like our position may meet less than hardy approval we tend to avoid explicit expression of that position. We waffle. It all started back there in the garden. Waffling is nothing new.

When the dragon/snake presented that God's verdict was possibly wrong , maybe even hiding something, and there was even benefit in crossing His word, her softening on the strict rule given turned into the fall. She took the fruit. It was tasty. She took another piece and took it to her husband. He too ate of it.

Then things started to go strange. When you look at the last verse of chapter 2 this little footnote is tossed in: "And they were both naked, the man and his wife, and were not ashamed." But after they broke the law of God, "...she took of its fruit and ate. She also gave to her husband with her, and he ate. Then the eyes of both of them were opened, and they knew that they were naked; and they sewed fig leaves together and made themselves coverings" Genesis 3:6, 7. It's still the case. We do something ill-advised and we feel sheepish, vulnerable to exposure. We start pulling things together to cover up. Can you see this scene? They suddenly are embarrassed, ashamed of themselves, they felt the cold of death approaching. They had to have a covering.

There were some large fig leaves nearby. Vines or tall grass was handy. Sewing was new to them. As the leaves wilted they became even more fragile. In fear they frantically laced the leaves together, perhaps accusation tinged sideways glances as they tried to learn from each other's progress. Then much to their chagrin "they heard the sound of the Lord God walking in the garden in the cool of the day, and Adam and his wife hid themselves from the presence of the Lord God among the trees of the garden" vs 8. God gently made His presence known. They weren't good at this hiding thing. The rustle gave them away as if God didn't already know their plight. Their makeshift attire took a serious hit.

"Then the Lord God called to Adam and said to him, 'Where are you?'

"So he said, 'I heard Your voice in the garden, and I was afraid because I was naked; and I hid myself.'"

What a pitiful sight came to view as Adam shyly shuffled into God's presence. The fearful, down cast demeanor; the effort to hang on to their disintegrating makeshift coverings which they soon gave up on and let pool about their feet. It was apparent that "there is no creature hidden from His sight, but all things are naked and open to the eyes of Him to whom we must give account" Hebrews 4:13. In dread their minds played "in the day that you eat of it you shall surely die." This is it. But what exactly was it? There had been no death before, what was death? It didn't sound good.

God opens an investigation in an effort to bring them back to their senses. "'Who told you that you were naked? Have you eaten from the tree of which I commanded you that you should not eat?'

"Then the man said, 'The woman whom You gave to be with me, she gave me of the tree, and I ate.'

"And the Lord God said to the woman, 'What is this you have done?

"The woman said, 'The serpent deceived me, and I ate'" Genesis 3:11-13.

"Yeah. But... But I was setup. It wasn't my fault. It was him or her or it. I was tricked. I was duped." With every opportunity we face we have at least one choice. Yes or No. Or even this, that, or else... in some setups. "No" had been a viable, a better, option. But they said "Yes" to the offer.

The man said, "The woman..."

The woman said, "The serpent..."

They both deflected responsibility. Is this so different from today?

God starts explaining the consequences of what just happened. To each of the players in this scene God says just a bit about what will happen. History fills in so much more.

"So the Lord God said to the serpent: 'Because you have done this, You are cursed more than all cattle, And more than every beast of the field; On your belly you shall go, And you shall eat dust All the days of your life'" Genesis 3:15. Sin degrades everything it touches. The serpent was among the most delightful of all creatures before he was possessed of the devil. Now it was cast down to disgust. The language implies this may have been an airborne creature as now it goes on its belly and its face is down in the dust. Indeed, scientists looking at snake skeletons say there is vestigial evidence of snakes having had limbs once, but sometime in the vast past they lost that. Could it have been here that it happened?

"And I will put enmity between you and the woman, And between your seed and her Seed; He shall bruise your head, And you shall bruise His heel" Genesis 3:15.

This appears to be a bit encrypted. When we link this with "So the great dragon was cast out, that serpent of old, called the Devil and Satan, who deceives the whole world" we realize God is addressing the one making the serpent talk (Revelation 12:9). This is the first prophecy of a showdown. Among the woman's offspring would come One who would be injured in the fight but Who would stomp his (Satan's) head. We can look back and see that God Himself will never be the same. The Creator would become a man born of the woman's seed. He would face Satan and take on some scars - as if becoming flesh and blood wasn't enough. But Satan would receive fatal injury from the encounter.

"To the woman He said: 'I will greatly multiply your sorrow and your conception; in pain you shall bring forth children; your desire shall be for your husband, and he shall rule over you'" Genesis 3:16.

The wonderful and natural process of childbirth would be quite uncomfortable, even possibly to risk of life itself. Raising children would be demanding. While all children would bring challenges, some would bring heartbreak. There is even implied a change in the length of time a woman could bear children. Where there would have been no death there was no need for a high birth rate. But now it would be necessary to extend childbearing to make up for losses due to death induced as a consequence of the new qualities of life.

There was a change in family structure. There would be a strong bond, a strong need of a good husband, a house-band. While it was strong before as in their being "one flesh," it would be different now. In a sense he would rule over her. That clause has been grossly misused, misunderstood, and abused. In the new order of things situations would develop where severe mediation in disagreements would be needed. Emergencies would arise. One person overseeing and directing appropriate action tends to manage confusion and enhance chances of recovery. Unfortunately, over the centuries, too often "the man of the house" looks after his own interests rather than overseeing the general welfare and success of the family enterprise and each of its members. As "house-band" he has a key role in the security and contentment of the family. When this gets distorted, marriage becomes less than desirable.

"Then to Adam He said, 'Because you have heeded the voice of your wife, and have eaten from the tree of which I commanded you, saying, *You shall not eat of it*: Cursed is the ground for your sake; in toil you shall eat of it all the days of your life. Both thorns and thistles it shall bring forth for you, and you shall eat the herb of the field. In the sweat of your face you shall eat bread till you return to the ground, for out of it you were taken; for dust you are, and to dust you shall return" Genesis 3:17-19.

God unloads on Adam. One verse is addressed to the woman. Three to the man. Though the woman found herself out of place near the tree and entertained the deceptive conversation, God tacitly accepted her plea of deception. God came down on Adam. He understood the fruit. He understood the contradiction of God's instruction. He was not deceived. He acted with knowledge and choice when he took the fruit. Now the nature of his work would be different, deliberate and hard. His nose was pointed to the ground. To this point their provisions came easily. Now nature would be disordered. Undesirable plants would encroach. Thorns, thistle, weeds, even rash inducing plants would infest his work space. Sweaty labor was now his lot. In due time even he would become the dirt he now had to work.

Note his nose is pointed to the soil. His primary role was to be provider. To a large degree he lost the right of dominion over operation of the earth. It no longer trusted and recognized him. The animals ran from him. The world went into a slow, sad decline until completion of the destruction by the flood.

At this point God's communication to them is brief - profound but brief. In their state of mind and inexperience their ability to process new information was limited. In time experience would make new guidance fitting and understandable.

"And Adam called his wife's name Eve, because she was the mother of all living" vs 20.

The very unity of Adam was broken. To this point God had not addressed the woman as Eve because he looked upon them as one flesh. To this point they were Adam, the race of people. In accepting Satan's proposition their unity was broken. Now the woman is given a new identity and a new name. Their oneness degrades to two people in a close relationship.

"In accepting Satan's proposition..." This is the key clause behind this record. This is why eating the delicious, beautiful fruit was so devastating. The fruit wasn't toxic; the proposition was toxic. On websites and in some other settings one may see a clause like this: "If you continue to use this site you accept the terms and the cookies of this site." If at that point I exit we're done. In eating the fruit they knowingly accepted the terms of the proposal (to be like God knowing good and evil) and his cookies which turned out be a deadly virus. The bite of the virus is quickly evidenced in their felt need to cover up. The sensed presence of God excites terror in them. They try to hide. They shun owning up to what they did: "She handed it to me..." "He gave it to me..." Don't blame me - I was set up. They knew they were in a bad site. They heard the proposition. They stuck around. They accepted the "cookies." Satan had been thrown out of heaven and the world was now his territory because he stole it. Eden, the garden home with its tree of life, was now fenced off. They were driven from this little taste of heaven called Eden, out into the undeveloped lands.

"Also for Adam and his wife the Lord God made tunics of skin, and clothed them" Genesis 3:21.

This short passage is phenomenally packed. They were standing there stunned, bewildered, dazed, guilty - and still naked. They were in need of cover-up. Their feeble attempt was wilted, disheveled about their feet.

The "age of grace" opens here. God has provided everything for them as He always had before. Now their need has increased immensely. God begins addressing a whole new, broad range of needs. "In the day that you eat of it you shall surely die" is put on hold. We are going to read into this passage a number of aspects implicit in this scene.

They had no idea what death was so He needed them to understand just what they had gotten themselves into with their actions. How best to do that? Where would "tunics of skin" come from? Nearby were a couple of animals - perhaps sheep. God reached out and touched one. It fell over and died. Eve may have played with that animal and I see her running over to it and finding it gone, no life in its eyes and she drew back horrified. Was this going to happen to them all?

God dressed it out, in front of them, quietly showing how it was done because now they would have to do that for themselves and for their children. He processed it into a leather gown and handed it to Eve. God selected another animal, processed it likewise into a suit for Adam. I can't imagine their shock. Two animals, probably pets standing near, were no more. They were wearing their skins. It is even likely the nature of animals changed and vultures arrived to clean up the mess of the animal's remnants. I can imagine Eve gagging as she watched the vultures tear into the carcass, and the flies joining in. Other animals came and introduced the sound of crunching bone. These are now a needful service to manage the pollution resulting from death. With a shudder, Adam turned away from the scene. Yet why did God chose to make leather for them?

Let's talk about leather. Years ago while feeding my interest in motorcycles I ran across an article about clothing as related to "road rash." A box was made that would hold some chalk. This box was attached to a truck in such a way that its bottom could be dragged along the road. Clothing material to be tested could be attached to the bottom of the box. The idea being that material failure would be marked by the point at which chalk appeared on the road as it was dragged along. Light cotton broke at about three feet. Denim made it maybe 10 feet. Kevlar, the stuff of bullet repelling vests, broke at 20. A nice, not particularly heavy leather jacket material slid down the road 70 feet before it broke through! God gave Adam and Eve available, tough, puncture and abrasion resistant attire. It was just what they needed. But they had to witness, even cause, death to obtain it. Can you imagine looking down at what you wore and seeing in your mind's eye an innocent sheep or goat?

Over time, they had over 900 years, they came to a startling realization on a whole new level; one they, and we, will likely marvel over and appreciate throughout eternity. From the sacrifice of a life they obtained a covering protecting them from the scrapes and jabs of everyday life. But they had another crucial, essential need - some way to handle their guilt, their treason to God's design and intention, their sin. Their covering for that would also come at the cost of life. It would cost the life of Someone they knew and loved - even worshiped. Their Creator was to become their Redeemer, their

Savior. They began to sort out the meaning of "He shall bruise your head And you shall bruise His heel." It must have been a keen, heart crushing moment when that thought sank into their awareness.

"Then the Lord God said, 'Behold, the man has become like one of Us, to know good and evil. And now, lest he put out his hand and take also of the tree of life, and eat, and live forever' — therefore the Lord God sent him out of the garden of Eden to till the ground from which he was taken. So He drove out the man; and He placed cherubim at the east of the garden of Eden, and a flaming sword which turned every way, to guard the way to the tree of life" Genesis 3:22-24.

Man is a created being. It was/is God's plan and desire that their life be permanent. We were supposed to be immortal. But as created beings their immortality was dependent; dependent on living within design parameters and on access to the Tree of Life. Eden is where the tree of life is located. So God fenced off access to the tree. Without its' vitalizing effect their life would wind down. When they saw what became of life as their children continued to do their own thing, as their bodies became more feeble they saw that death was actually a welcome state. Death in a broken world was really another gracious gift God provided. Even in this death God provided hope of salvation, restoration of what was lost. God has a plan whereby, "Blessed are those who do His commandments, that they may have the right to the tree of life, and may enter through the gates into the city" Revelation 22:14. Those who avail themselves of God's provision for recovery will share the city with Him and again have access to the tree of life. God's love induced Him to put the death sentence on hold, He devised and implemented a way to recovery. He exercises grace and mercy to provide space and time for recovery. But also in that space and time would come opportunity to thoroughly examine the "evil" of the proposition.

Chapter 7

Unity

"Then God said, 'Let Us make man in Our image...'" Genesis 1:26. It is well we take a moment to look into that "Us" and "Our." In the chapter "Creative Rampage" we touched on the plural pronouns a bit. There is more to look at and I'd like to go into that before we close down this study.

A movie I don't mind seeing again is "A Leap of Faith." Rick is young juvenile delinquent with a background in horses who finds himself as a stable hand in a summer camp for blind children and youth. One of his charges is Billy a shy 12 something boy who was blind from birth. Rick befriends Billy and teaches him to enjoy riding. One day Rick was leading a group on a trail. Along the ride Billy asks, "What color is my horse?" "Well, it's brown." "What does brown look like?" What can be said? His eyes have never worked. Color is indescribable to one who has never seen.

There are many ideas we will try to make sense of. But it will be kind of like trying to describe brown to a person whose eyes have never seen. But like the blind boy perhaps we can feel the horse and develop some sense of what a horse is like.

How can God (singular) address Himself by a plural pronoun? How can a man and woman be addressed as Adam? Why bother trying to bend our heads around such seemingly inane, incomprehensible questions?

First God provided us minds. Those minds have curiosity. Those minds desire to understand. Once we have a handle on one idea then we go "what about that?" As understanding develops in a variety of topics threads among topics begin to form and it gets more interesting to gnaw on puzzling things and link ideas together. Calculus is meaningless to someone trying figure out what numbers are and how they relate to reality. In time basic arithmetic expands to more abstract algebra. Then the once concrete, exacting calculations give way to making sense of the fuzzy ideas of statistics. So even as we study God and our place in His presence our understanding is able to stretch, enlarge, deepen.

Next God intended the life, and love He embedded in it, to be permanent. When it broke He never wanted to ball it up and throw it away or simply "uncreate" it. He wanted to fix the break. The term "salvation" is what we call fixing the break. As we work our way toward salvation it is helpful to try to understand what it is like to be fixed. What does "fixed" look like? We have already spent some ink on what once was because that is helpful in understanding what we can be - what we are to become.

The singular plurality idea is one of the first and key ideas we are exposed to in the Biblical record. Remember the Venn diagram on the back cover? We need to stand in front of a mirror and look at ourselves. We also look back over our shoulder and see at least something of God. A mirror has boundaries. It doesn't let us see the whole picture. What is does let us see can be very valuable.

We can understand apples and oranges better if we set them both in front of us and find similarities and differences. Both are fruit. Both grow on trees. Both are juicy but in different ways. They are both generally round. The apple is dimpled top and bottom. The orange is more textured. One puts its seeds in a core. The other near the apex of segments. Many more comparisons could be made. In those comparisons we become increasingly aware of the qualities of both. If all we had were apples there would be qualities of the apple we probably would miss without something else with which to compare.

Using what is in the Bible and some of our experience we are going to, in a sense, be in front of a mirror comparing the likeness of ourselves with God. This will help us work through what was, what is meant to be, what is, what needs to be fixed. This is an ongoing study. We can only streak the surface dust here.

"So God created man in His own image; in the image of God He created him; male and female He created them" Genesis 1:27. "...a man shall leave his father and mother and be joined to his wife, and they shall become one flesh" Genesis 2:24. So originally man and wife became a single entity. The likes of which we have never seen but in our nature to seek to regain. One aspect of this is the tradition of the wife's name changing to the family name of her husband. Her identity becomes closely linked to his.

But what of the persons comprising God? There are a few passages in the Bible that can help us but perhaps the most succinct is Matthew 28:19, "Go therefore and make disciples of all the nations, baptizing them in the name of the Father and of the Son and of the Holy Spirit." Here we have the singular name and titles for the constituents. Many volumes have been written by PhDs trying to sort this out. Refer again to the Venn diagram on the cover. Note the large common area. This area contains the fundamental nature of love, grace, hopes, desires, etc. that is God. Yet each member of Godhead has different roles.

The distinctive role of the Father is perhaps the least well understood to us. Jesus said when he was here, "I and My Father are one" John 10:30. In chapters 14 through 17 Jesus says more about the association of Himself and Father. Drawing from the human likeness, a good father and husband oversees his household in a way that provides a family identity, many needs, a sense of security, of helping coordinate opportunities and goals. We see a likeness between the Father and the human father.

The female aspect of humanity is identified as an aspect of the image - the likeness - of God. Let's peruse that for a moment. "Now Adam knew Eve his wife, and she conceived and bore Cain..." Genesis 4:1. Together a child was conceived. "She conceived and bore" a child. " For by Him all things were created that are in heaven and that are on earth, visible and invisible, whether thrones or dominions or principalities or powers. All things were created through Him and for Him. And He is before all things, and in Him all things consist" Colossians 1:16, 17. God conceived creation. God conceived us. All of creation came into existence through Christ. As the child comes into existence of the woman, the wife: creation came to exist through Christ. They are the agent who brings into existence. So women hold a particular likeness to Christ. When God said "Let Us make...", they conceived and Christ brought it into existence. Their methodology is different but the resemblance is there.

By design women nurture in ways men can't. Men can't nurse, cuddle and nurture in womanly ways. But men's grumble, sometimes growl, and have a tendency to rough and tumble which brings comfort and contentment in ways women can't muster; especially for their sons. They're protective of their daughters and it makes them feel safe.

Though men and women are different they love, they share, they complement and complete each other's qualities to a beautiful, fulfilling unity. The unity of God is complimentary, completing, fulfilling. There is to be a complimentary, completing, fulfilling unity between God and man. Much of the rest of this work, this "systematic theology," is an effort to understand and aid in recovery of the intended fulfilling unity among us and between God and man.

The Holy Spirit does not get much mention in Scripture. We are told one of His titles is the Comforter, the one who brings unity and power to the church and His people. In the very first verse of the Bible Genesis 1:1-2, the Spirit is mentioned. "In the beginning God created the heavens and the earth. The earth was without form, and void; and darkness was on the face of the deep. And the **Spirit of God** was hovering over the face of the waters." Other versions say it was brooding over the waters. You get a feeling of a woman about to give birth, or someone making something creative, studying it, taking a deep breath as they begin something, getting ready to turn fabric into a quilt, or bare wood into a carving. In Psalms 33:6, we are told by the singer, "By the word of the Lord the heavens were made, and all the host of them by the breath [Spirit] of His mouth." Mary, mother of Jesus was told at the conception of Christ "The Holy Spirit will come upon you, and the power of the Highest will overshadow you" Luke 1:35. It appears whenever God is about to do something creative, wondrous, powerful, the Spirit is present.

In other places, the Spirit is called our helper. For instance, John 14:26 "But the Helper, the Holy Spirit, whom the Father will send in My name, He will teach you all things, and bring to your remembrance all things that I said to you." Once Christ returned to heaven, the Spirit came and began his work here as our teacher and provider and the one who deals directly with His broken children.

As we look at the singular plurality of God and consider Their likeness in us, can we perhaps see an aspect of the Holy Spirit represented in our design? As our children were growing up it was apparent that generally Mother was where they went for comfort and help. As they got a little older there were some things they came to me for. Now we are grandparents. When the kids call and I answer the phone often times they hear me and "Is Mom there?" happens. I get the call if the car's broke. Mom gets the call if it's the hearts breaking. So we both have our sphere of comfort and help but Mom holds the larger side of that role.

[1] There is an interesting observation to be drawn from the genealogy of Jesus as recorded in Luke 3. He goes through the tree. "...the son of Joseph, the son of Heli, the son of Matthat, the son of Levi... Adam the son of God."

Chapter 8

Closure Thoughts

I took a low level physics class in college. The professor had the wisdom to use a text that approached the development of the concepts on a historical perspective. I learned so much the process of discovery. The simple basic concepts were easy to grasp. When those ideas ran into difficulty refinements of history made sense and organized physics into a logical line of development. Eventually lines between observations began to form and a whole new line of science would appear in history and in my head. It all developed rather naturally over the centuries.

I have attempted to implement that model of historical development. The historical approach begins to expose how "God is love" permeates everything. We have considered that His love is the rationale behind the creative rampage that was our beginnings. While He has ultimate capability in all senses of the word, He is personable. His love is not tyrannically demanding. His love is voluntarily extended. He desires our love to voluntarily circulate. He provided much opportunity for choice and creativity, even bad choices. His love is so personable that He exhibited grace to stall justice so time and opportunity for recovery became available. This was all seen in broad and general strokes.

Part two of this work will look at some specifics in greater detail. In our studies in these short volumes, we will endeavor to say make religion be less of "do as you are told" and more a matter of "this is how it works. You apply it as you are led." And always , always, "How is this next idea an expression or aspect of God's love?"

About the Author:

Dan Pelton's first home was a 400 acre farm in the little village of Langon, New Hampshire. Those first six years left a profound mark on him. When he was three his parents met Christianity. Except for one year in a technical community college all of his formal education has been in Christian schools. He notes "formal education." For a few formative years his father worked as a custodian in a public library. Dan discovered the 500 (science) and 600 (technology) sections, first devouring the juvenile area and making serious inroads into the adult area when he could sneak in. His private labs for study of electricity, electronics, optics, carpentry, mechanics, model aircraft scattered around the house, garage, basement. He got a little training on the piano and organ as well, plays the verrillon on occasion (tuned water glasses) and even played bass viol for a while in high school and college.

His mild dyslexia made writing a challenge. Yet he discovered that sketching and writing were rewarding in understanding and refining ideas. Once he obtained a computer, writing was less a chore and became a means to keep ideas in place. His social life was distinctly flavored by both Asperger's traits and his conservative Christian parents.

Dan tends to discover questions and deliberately gnaw on them toward satisfying answers. This has served him well for 40+ years of working as a technician in equipment service, repair, and research and development.

In the mid-80s a significant chunk of his curiosity and creativity turned to matters of theology. Several significant things converged at that time. A computer became available as a writing prosthetic. He was asked to serve a significant position in the local congregation he attended. In the first week of service he opened a study: Church – Why Bother? Over time more questions, puzzles, and ideas were subjected to the crucible of writing. As the body of work developed his wife began suggesting some of it be collected so others could look at it.

Along the way God saw to it that he earn a BA in Theology.

"God is love" is a phrase he grew up with. Then a few years ago he began to realize the massive implications of that statement. It time it "became the sun around which all teaching, indeed, existence itself orbited." He grew up in a "this is what the Bible says. Do as it says" framework. Now he is rebuilding the framework, finding freedom in the magnificence of God's plan and he's beginning to make some of his thoughts available for the consideration of others.

Our Invitation:

Thank you so for reading this little book, written for the glory of God. I hope you will take the time to go to God, if you haven't already, and take advantage of His free gift. Your prayer does not have to be fancy. It can be something as simple as this:

Dear God, I know that I am a sinner and there is nothing that I can do to save myself. I confess my complete helplessness to forgive my own sin or to work my way to righteousness. At this moment I trust Christ alone as the One who bore my sin when He died on the cross. I believe that He did all that will ever be necessary for me to stand in your holy presence. Thank you for sending your Son to die in my place. I am grateful that He has promised to accept me just as I am right now. Father, I take you at your word. I believe you are my Lord and Creator and God. Thank you for the assurance that you will walk with me through all my life and even my death. Thank you for hearing this prayer and making me your child. Lead me in the way you would have me go from this time forward.. In Jesus' Name. Amen.

If you pray this prayer, or one like it, please contact me on my website and let me know. I'd love to send you some information to help you on your new life path.

Our publisher webpage address is:

Travelerpelton.com

Our facebook is travelerpelton

Dan is available at **great.commission@aol.com**

He would love to hear from you.

While you're visiting us on our website or FB page, I hope you take the time to get acquainted with us, the writers at Potpourri Publishing .

And remember our invitation; when we get to heaven, at that last day, you'll find the tree of life spanning the river of life. The first Sabbath, we will be with Jesus and the Father and our angel celebrating our first Sabbath in heaven. The second Sabbath, we will be with our family, all the generations back, again, celebrating,. But that next Sabbath is for all of us. On the third Sabbath after we get there, we're all meeting on the left bank for a potluck and to share our stories. We'd be pleased if you'd join us there. It's going to be grand! We can't wait to meet all of you who may have gotten to know Him better from reading our books.. May God bless you forever.

To our friends:

You can reach Traveler or Dan at her website:

travelerpelton.com

Or like us and share us on **Facebook at Traveler Pelton**

Or write to her by **snail mail** at

Springhaven Croft

212 Sychar Rd.

Mt. Vernon, OH 43050

She and Dan loves to hear from her readers!

All our books are available on Amazon as both eBook and print copy, Kindle Unlimited as free downloads

We'd love it if you'd leave us a review! It helps others find our books.

God bless and see you in our next travels together!

100

Your Attention Please!!!!

<u>Would you like to join the team at Potpourri Books?</u>

Traveler is <u>always</u> looking for responsible beta readers for her new books. A beta reader gets a prepublication copy of all new books, <u>free of charge</u> in exchange for an honest review written on Amazon, and a short email letting her know of any glitches you may have found that got past the editor, any suggestions you may have, and your opinion of the book. What else do you get out of it?

A beta reader gets:

A free download of one of her already published books and

as soon as your review of that book gets placed on Amazon,

free downloads of her already published works: for each review, you get a free book.

And

A free copy pre publication copy of all new books…

And

Other neat freebies as they come, from bookmarks to stickers to posters to pens to neat things I find to send out to my betas-

Interested?

Contact Traveler at

<u>travelerpelton@gmail.com</u> for more info…

We would love to add you to the team!

While Dan is working on his next book, perhaps you would enjoy the devotional just put out by J. Traveler Pelton, his wife and fellow Christian author. It's from her book, Natural Morning.

Therefore by the deeds of the law no flesh will be justified in His sight, for by the law is the knowledge of sin. (Romans 3:20)

Are you saved because of your actions? Many people seem to believe that we are saved by being good, and as a result are trying hard to earn brownie points with God. Are you lost because of your bad deeds? Are you lost because you do bad things? The answer is no. You're not saved or lost because of your behavior. You are saved or lost because of your love for Christ, which shines through in your behaviors. Let me tell you a story.

Once a very pompous person was trying to impress upon a bunch of kids the importance of living a clean Christian life. He held forth at great length about the extreme importance in making a good impression, looking the part, smiling properly, neat hair, proper language, the entire package.

Then he drew himself up to his full height, looked down his nose at the boys and said, "Why do people call me a Christian?"

"I don't know," said one boy. "Maybe it's because they don't know you."

Ouch! Was the man a Christian? Well, he thought he

was. His behavior, to his mind, was exemplary. But the boys had his show all figured out. With his example, they remained unconverted. He wasn't showing Christ. He was showing himself.

A person who doesn't know Christ and has not accepted His salvation is simply lost. He isn't lost because he does bad things; he does bad things because he doesn't know Christ, and is therefore lost.

A good person who doesn't know Christ is just as lost as the man dealing drugs on the street or a person who deliberately murders people. If you don't have Christ, it's irrelevant what you do with your life. It's all going to just burn up in the end like so much tinder.

Knowing Christ saves people. He is our only righteousness.

"Believing the right things about Jesus isn't enough. You're not adopted as God's child until you confess and turn away from your wrongdoing and receive the freely offered gift of forgiveness and eternal life that Jesus purchased with his death on the cross. Until you do that, you'll always be on the outside looking in."

Lee Stroebel

Another book Coming out in May from Traveler Pelton is tentatively titled <u>Ninety Days to The God Habit</u>: this is just the introduction to a very hands on book about you finding your path to a better knowledge of the God Dan speaks of ion his work, the God that is love:

Introduction

If you are reading this book, I am assuming the idea of getting closer to God in just a few short weeks has intrigued you, whetted your appetite. You may be a searcher, or someone dissatisfied with a lukewarm state of soul or someone who has long walked with Him and feel that for some reason nothing is working anymore. At any rate, you have tried and failed to set up anything that has worked to bring you closer to God and the peace of mind that brings. You may think the routine of daily life does not allow you time to bring yourself in sync with God; there are not enough hours in the day to pray and study and keep up with everything and that leaves you feeling dissatisfied and upset. Whatever the reason, you are looking for some way, some reason, some formula or schematic or equation to make the unease go away. I felt that way once and what I learned about escaping that feeling is the rationale behind this book.

Among the roles I fill in my life are Wife, Mother, Grandmother, church planter, shepherd, farmer, writer and Social Worker. The ways people live their lives endlessly fascinates me. I never have quite enough time to read all the journal studies done about people. I do try, and I find that it's hard to comb through all the jargon to find small nuggets of truth that I find useful in my work in counseling and coaching people. Over the years, the gleaning and application of what I learn to what people who come to me need is a cause and effect sort of serendipity that is like music playing; you know it works, but unless you're the orchestra conductor or the composer you are never quite sure how it goes together, it simply does and it makes the listening a pleasure. The aha! moments I see in my office as something clicks within people is a pleasure. I like to see it happen so I keep track of what seems to be the most problematic for my patients and for my church members and then I go into research mode to find answers for them and in doing so, often find it helps me as well.

A short while back, I got very interested in habits; habits are automatic behaviors that have been wired into our brains through repetition; I wanted to find out what it takes to make them, what it takes to break them, how we can control them. Too many of the people I saw were struggling with stopping the consequences of habits they'd made early in life and now were paying for, yet felt helpless to do anything. Their habits were killing them. They'd developed them early in life and they wanted them to go away. They wouldn't go easily without a struggle.

It's a little like taming lions. When a lion is little, (or so I am told. I do not raise lions, only children, alpaca, Pomeranians, canaries and Siamese cats) when a lion is less than three months old, they are cuddly and easy to play with and they are simple to get away from. You stand up, slip them off your lap and walk away. They may give chase but they really aren't all that hurtful. When a lion grows larger, say nine months, they are much more determined, stronger, and it might take someone helping you, interceding as it were, to get away from a determined young lion. You'll come away with bites, scratches and a determination not to go in that cage again. But once a lion is full grown, you need someone with a gun or a tranquilizer gun to slow it down or kill it outright and you will not get out unscathed. You will get hurt. You could even die. The same is true for habits. You can smoke a cigarette or a joint once or twice with friends and put it down. You can overindulge on alcohol, or tell white lies, or cheat on your taxes and probably get away with it for a time. You can neglect to pray daily, and think to come back to it. If time goes on, and you continue to smoke, the poisons that are addictive get stronger and harder to overcome. You can still stop doing it, but you may need some help, like nicotine patches, a support group or a good scare from your doctor.

Just the same, if you have neglected God for some time, you are going to put some effort into getting back into His throne room, feeling comfortable with His presence again. Do not think I am saying He has left you; no, but just as any other earthly friend, you can drift apart and the first steps back into friendship feel awkward; after asking about the job, and the kids and the weather, what do you talk about? You can restart your spiritual life, you can regain the place you once held in His presence and feel His help, but you may need some prodding from someone who loves you. He knew that and He sent us his Holy Spirit to get us to remember just when we need it. (John 14:26 But the Helper, the Holy Spirit, whom the Father will send in My name, He will teach you all things, and bring to your remembrance all things that I said to you.)

I know from experience, the longer you let it wait, put it aside, and think I'll do it tonight, or tomorrow morning, or when Lent comes or it's going to be my New Years' resolution next year, you come to the place where it seems too hard, there are simply too many reason to not read the Bible, or think of Him, or talk to Him. You have officially drifted and eventually that Old Serpent will whisper you've gone too far, it's too hard, you're too busy, nobody does that anymore and you wander into a complacent mode. You know you're a Christian although you can't quite remember to call on Him when needed, or where that verse in the Bible was that you need right now, and your soul somewhat closes its spiritual eyes and goes to sleep. The Spirit , in an attempt to wake you up, sometimes resorts to extreme measures to wake you up, and sometimes, even that doesn't work anymore. Has God moved? No, you lost anchor, you are out to sea and you need rescued. When it gets that far, you need a complete revival, a re-doing of your habits, a turning back, repentance if you will, in order to regain that first love, that flush of affection, that security that He is there for you. Sometimes something out of the ordinary comes along and you suddenly realize you've neglected Him so much you're afraid to talk to Him. Then the cancer comes or the car wreck, or the marriage problems, and you find yourself lost with no one to comfort you and you wonder where is God? He didn't go anywhere. You wandered. The fact that you have gotten a copy of this book may be a leading of the Spirit to bring you closer to Him. This book is written to help you find your straight path out of the bad habit of ignoring the Lord of the Universe and engaging in behavior that will being you closer to heaven. This book will help you develop a habit of putting God first and accepting His leading and His rewards.

So if you're trying to get back to Him, or perhaps you never knew Him in the first place, or perhaps you're a new believer and wanted to make changes in the right way, whichever is the case, let me assure you, He is a gentleman, He is a lover, He is still there waiting for you to make an appointment with Him every day. The question you ask me is simple: how do I get from point A-which is where I am to point B, where I want to be, in the shortest, fastest way possible? I am glad you asked. With a prayer and a song, let's begin our odyssey, the pilgrimage we are beginning to activate our God Habit.

Other books from our Authors!

Books by Traveler Pelton

Spiritual Works
- God Wanted to Write a Bestseller
- Big God, Little Me
- Lenten Stories for God's Little Children
- Natural Morning
- Ninety Days to The God Habit

Literary Christian Science Fiction
The First Oberllyn Family Trilogy: The Past

- The Oberllyn's Overland: 1855-1862
- Terrorists, Traitors and Spies 1900-1990
- Rebooting the Oberllyn's 2015-2020

The Second Oberllyn Family Trilogy: The Present

- The Infant Conspiracy
- Kai Dante's Stratagem
- The Obligation of Being Oberllyn

The Third Oberllyn Family Trilogy: The Future

- To Protect One's Own
- The Importance of Family Ties
- Kith and Kin, Together Again

Family History
- Journey to Springhaven

**Traveler In Collaboration with T. Bear Pelton:
(He writes Christian fantasy)**
- <u>Clan Falconer's War</u>
- <u>The Rise of the Rebellion</u>
- <u>Changeling's Clan</u>

From Lynette Spencer

- <u>Basic Sewing on a Budget</u>
- <u>Vegetarian Cooking on a Budget</u>

Thank you and God bless from all of us here at Potpourri Publishing!

Take time to work, it is the price of success.
Take time to think, it is the source of power.
Take time to play, it is the secret of perpetual youth.
Take time to read, it is the fountain of wisdom.
Take time to be friendly, it is the road to happiness.
Take time to dream, it is hitching your wagon to a star.
Take time to look around, it is too short a day to be selfish.
Take time to laugh, it is the music of the soul.

~ Old English Prayer

Made in the USA
Coppell, TX
26 April 2020